one page at a time...

your grief matters

your grief matters

your grief matters

This journal belongs to:

_____

in loving memory of:

_____

MAGNOLIA
MEMORIAL

TODAY, TOMORROW, ALWAYS

Forever in my Heart

4X6" PHOTO

date:

Introduce your loved one

....

....

....

....

....

....

....

....

....

....

....

draw/describe
My grief support system is...

your life was a

blessing

your memory a

Treasure

you are loved beyond

words

and missed beyond

measure

What helps you cope with your grief?

What are three words to describe your grief?

1.

2

3.

date:

I am proud of you for...

....

....

....

....

....

....

....

....

....

....

....

PHOTO

09 00 47 28
TRAVEL STAMP

your life gave us

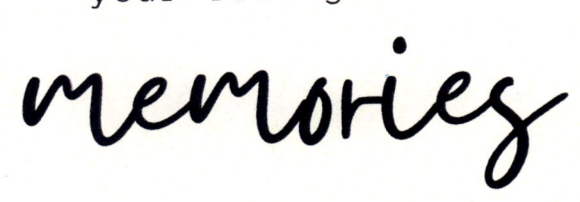

memories

too beautiful to forget

I grieve the should haves

I grieve the could haves

I grieve the would haves

MY GRIEF CALENDAR

CIRCLE YOUR GRIEF DAYS

Month _____

1	2	3	4	5	6	7
8	9	10	11	12	13	14
15	16	17	18	19	20	21
22	23	24	25	26	27	28
29	30	31				

these are my grief days because:

_____
_____
_____
_____

date:

Today, I am really missing...

···
···
···
···
···
···
···
···
···
···
···
···

THE WORLD CHANGES
FROM YEAR TO YEAR,
OUR LIVES FROM DAY
TO DAY, BUT THE LOVE
AND MEMORY OF YOU,
SHALL NEVER PASS
AWAY

ACTS OF SELF LOVE
TO SHOW MYSELF TODAY:

- ♥ REFLECT & WRITE

- ♥ PRACTICE MEDITATION

- ♥ UNPLUG FROM SOCIAL MEDIA

- ♥
- ♥
- ♥
- ♥

date:

I can't help but smile when I think about the time...

....

....

....

....

....

....

....

....

....

....

....

SAY THEIR NAME

SAY THEIR NAME

SAY THEIR NAME

HELLO, I'm grieving because I miss

date:

The funniest thing
I remember about you is...

Reminder

Grief has no timeline.

draw a face to show how you are feeling today

I miss you

I miss YOU

I MISS YOU

GRIEF AFFIRMATIONS

- ♥ I can feel happy today

- ♥ I can take comfort in my memories

- ♥ I will allow myself to feel feelings

- ♥

- ♥

- ♥

date:

write a letter to your loved one

....

....

....

....

....

....

....

....

....

....

....

draw/describe
The most challenging time of day is...

color/circle
Where in my body am I feeling this grief?

Reminder

I am not selfish for taking time to myself. It is okay to focus on myself.

MY GRIEF PLAYLIST

MY FAVORITE QUOTES

" "

" "

" "

MY FAVORITE QUOTES

"   "

"   "

"   "

date:

I wish I would have told you...

....
....
....
....
....
....
....
....
....
....
....
....

you are
loved

you are
missed

you are
remembered

draw/describe
Some of my grief triggers are...

describe/list
What do you wish others knew about your grief?

date:

I miss talking to you about...

....

....

....

....

....

....

....

....

....

....

....

GRIEF IS LIKE THE OCEAN;
IT COMES IN WAVES,
EBBING AND FLOWING.
SOMETIMES THE WATER IS
CALM, AND SOMETIMES IT
IS OVERWHELMING. ALL WE
CAN DO IS LEARN TO SWIM.

—VICKI HARRISON

OCEAN WAVES

COLOR AND LABEL THE BIG WAVES BELOW
WITH THE BIG EMOTIONS THAT YOU ARE FEELING

draw/describe
How are you feeling today?

date:

I always laughed when you...

....

....

....

....

....

....

....

....

....

....

....

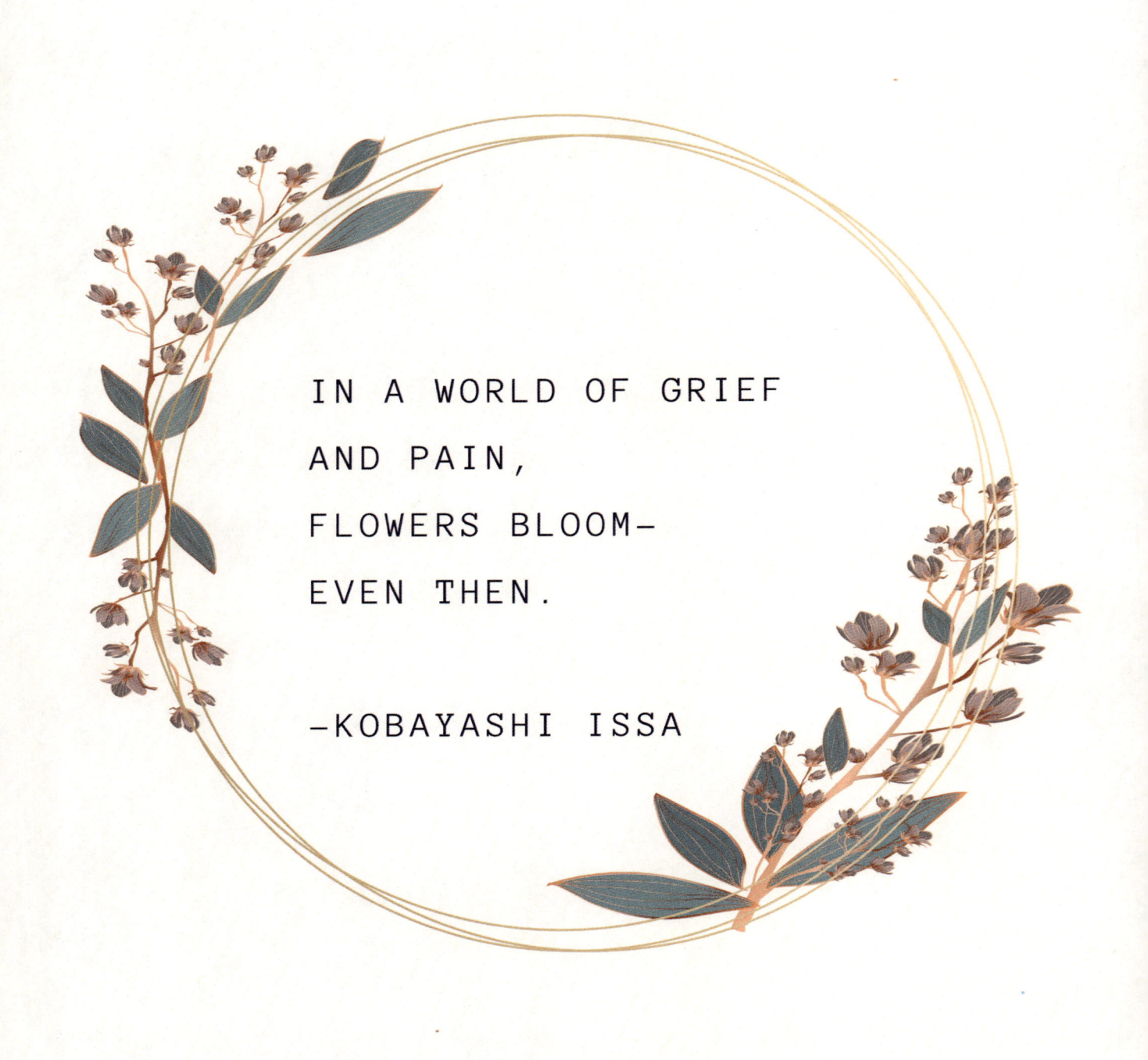

IN A WORLD OF GRIEF
AND PAIN,
FLOWERS BLOOM—
EVEN THEN.

—KOBAYASHI ISSA

color the vase and add flowers
to show how you are feeling

YOUR LOVED ONES FAVORITE
ARTISTS/BANDS/ SONGS/MUSIC

-
-
-
-
-
-

There are some
who bring a
light so great
to the world
that even after
they have gone
the light
remains

date:

If I could talk to you again, I'd tell you...

....

....

....

....

....

....

....

....

....

....

....

....

A BUTTERFLY TO REMIND ME

EVEN THOUGH WE ARE APART

YOUR SPIRIT IS ALWAYS WITH ME

FOREVER IN MY HEART

YOUR LOVED ONES FAVORITE
RESTARUANTS/FOODS/CANDY/DESSERTS

-
-
-
-
-

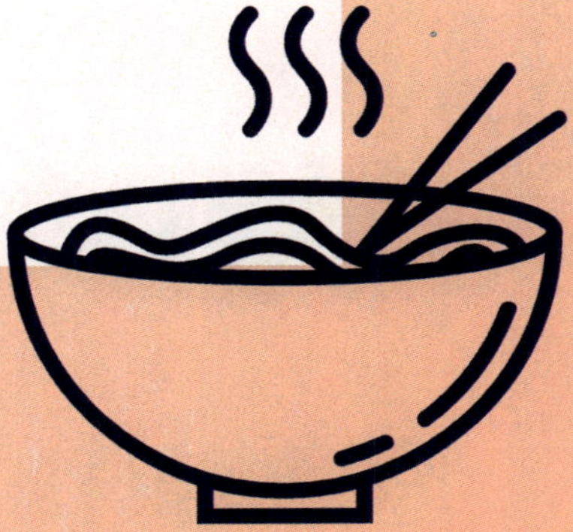

draw/describe
When I think about you I feel...

"

"

color the face to show
how you are feeling today

Reminder

My grief and emotions are valid and I will not dismiss them.

date:

My most difficult memory of you is...

....

....

....

....

....

....

....

....

....

....

....

....

draw/describe
What emotions do you feel
looking back at these memories?

Things to remember today:

♥   My grief is valid

♥   Rest is productive

♥

♥

♥

FEELINGS STORM

circle your feelings

RESENTFULL

APPREHENSIVE

CALM

IRATE GLOOMY

DESPERATE

FUMING

LOW

AFRAID

MEH CROSS

BLEAK

OUTRAGED

ANXIOUS

ANGER

FEAR DEPRESSED

RATTY

MISERABLE

ANNOYED SAD

draw/list
What do you wish others knew about your grief?

date:

one of my fondest
memories
of you:

....

....

....

....

....

....

....

....

....

....

....

There are no goodbyes for us. Wherever you are, you will always be in my heart.

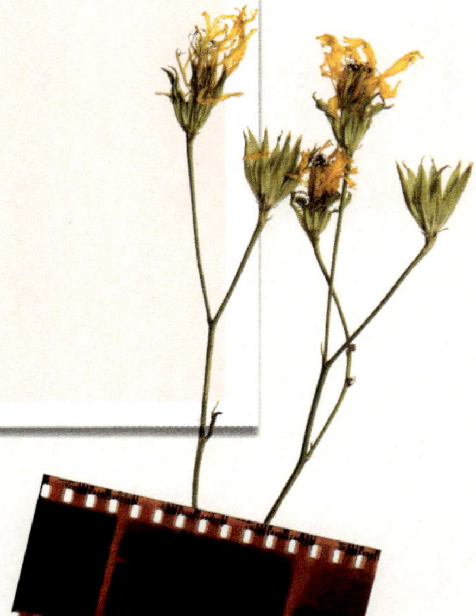

Reminder

Your journey is your own.

date:

What are you grateful for today?

....

....

....

....

....

....

....

....

....

....

....

blank pages for you to
journal, doodle, scrap-book:
article/magazine clippings, pictures,
letters, receipts, tickets, etc.

thank you
FOR SUPPORTING OUR SMALL FAMILY BUSINESS

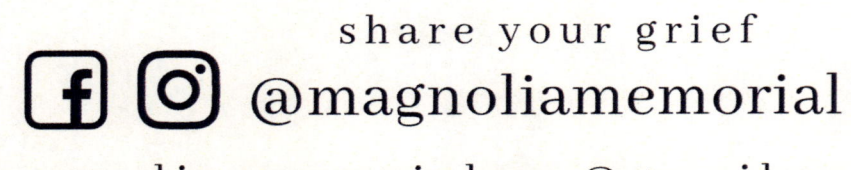

CREATED WITH LOVE BY

MAGNOLIA
MEMORIAL

share your grief
@magnoliamemorial

magnoliamemorialusa@gmail.com

Made in the USA
Las Vegas, NV
11 September 2023